Dedication

To my wonderful husband, whose love and support make every challenge lighter and every joy sweeter—thank you for being my rock and my partner in this beautiful, messy journey.

To my amazing kids, who inspire me every day with your curiosity, laughter, and growing independence—may you always chase your dreams with courage and kindness.

This book is for you guys, my greatest adventure.

Table of Contents

KINDA FINE, KINDA LOSING IT

A Fun and Honest Look at Mom Life, Identity, and the Weird Middle Years

By Becky Miller

Table of Contents Continued

Table of Contents Continued

Preface

You're Not Alone, Even if It Feels Like It

This is not a book to fix you.

 You don't need fixing.

You need someone to sit beside you for a moment and say, "You're not imagining this. And you're not alone."

Maybe life looks fine on paper—everyone's healthy, you've kept them alive another day, the house isn't falling apart (well, not completely), and dinner usually happens. But still, something feels...off. Not wrong exactly. Just a little dull, a little stuck. Like your spark wandered off and forgot to come back.

This book was born in that space.

I didn't write it from the mountaintop. I wrote it from my living room—after dropping the kids off at jiu jitsu, coming home to a quiet house, and realizing I didn't feel like myself anymore. I wasn't sad, exactly. I wasn't even overwhelmed. I just felt blah. Lost in a life I loved but didn't quite recognize.

And the more I looked around, the more I realized: this feeling is everywhere. Especially for women who have spent years pouring into their families, homeschooling, homemaking, caring, creating—and suddenly find themselves in a season where things are quieter, but not necessarily easier. The kids still need you, but not like they used to. Your days are full, but your heart feels a little empty.

This is the middle.

Not the shiny beginning when everything is exciting and new.

Not the triumphant end where you finally feel like you figured it all out.

 Just the middle—messy, quiet, confusing, beautiful, and real.

So no, you're not broken.
You're just shifting.
Becoming.
Re-orienting your life around a center that's moving.

And that deserves tenderness. Compassion. And maybe a few laughs along the way.

This isn't a to-do list or a glow-up plan. It's a warm conversation. A soft place to land. A handful of reminders that you are still here, still whole, and still wildly worthy— even if your days don't feel all that extraordinary.

I hope you find yourself in these pages—not a new version of you, but the one who's been quietly waiting for a little more space to breathe.

So let's begin—with the moment I realized I needed this book just as much as anyone else.

1

Why I'm Even Writing This

The Blah That Started It All

It started with jiu jitsu.

Well, technically, it started with me sitting at my computer after dropping the kids off at jiu jitsu. My husband teaches the class, so I didn't even need to stay. I came home to a quiet condo, sat down at my wall-mounted computer desk in the bedroom with my fresh cup of tea, and just... stared at the screen.

I wasn't sad. Not really.

Everything in my life was "fine"—like, actually fine. The kids were healthy. School was going smoothly. My marriage was solid. Even my body, which has a track record of betraying me, was mostly cooperating. I had time to write, time to breathe, time to rest. And yet something felt wrong.

Not dramatically wrong—just off. Blah. Flat. Like the colors had faded a little bit.

I wanted to work on a new children's book. I usually love that—creating whimsical stories, playful illustrations, something for parents and kids to enjoy together. But the motivation just wasn't there. I didn't feel inspired or excited. I wasn't drowning... I just wasn't sparkling, either.

So I did what most modern, overwhelmed women do: I asked the internet what was wrong with me.

I typed how I was feeling into ChatGPT. (Yes, really.) I didn't expect much, maybe a "you're burned out, drink more water" kind of answer. But what I got instead? It made me cry.

It described exactly what I was feeling. Like someone had finally put words to this weird fog I was stuck in. That's when I realized—maybe I wasn't the only one.

So I started writing. Not a children's book, not a how-to guide, not a "here's how to be a better mom" list. I just started writing all the things I needed to hear. Because maybe—just maybe—someone else needed to hear them too.

Who This Book Is For

I'm writing to the woman who's been at home for years, teaching her kids, making snacks, building memories—

who genuinely loves being a mom and a homemaker. You've homeschooled, or unschooled, or afterschooled... you've done the whole hands-on thing. You've built your life around your family.

But now?

Your kids are older. Maybe middle schoolers, maybe teens. They can manage their own homework. They log into their online classes without reminders (most of the time). They stay up late reading fantasy novels or texting friends, and nobody needs you to read Goodnight Moon anymore.

You still love this life, but the rhythm has changed—and you didn't realize how disorienting that would be. You feel like you went from being the sun in everyone's orbit to... a dependable minivan with snacks and Wi-Fi.

You're still needed, but not in the same way.

Why I'm The One Writing It

I've been home with my kids every single day since my youngest was born. My health challenges made full-time work impossible, and childcare costs made it impractical. So I leaned all the way in. We cooked together, we read together, we learned together. Our days were full of snuggles and experiments and library hauls that broke the bag straps.

And now?

They still need me—but differently. I'm a chauffeur. A calendar manager. An occasional assignment checker. I'm the voice reminding them it's time for class or that shoes exist and should be worn in public.

And when you've spent a decade being everything to small people, that shift can make you feel... lost.
Not depressed. Not miserable. Just adrift. Like, who am I if I'm not needed every minute?

What This Book Isn't

This isn't a book about grieving your kids growing up. Honestly, I love watching them become more independent. I'm so proud of who they're becoming, and I can't wait to see where they go.

This isn't about wanting them little again—it's about not knowing who you are now that they're not little.

This isn't a productivity pep talk. I'm not going to tell you to start a business, redecorate your house, or launch a new version of yourself. (Unless you want to, in which case—go for it!)

This book is about finding peace and purpose in the middle. It's for the moms who are still home, still giving, still deeply invested in their families—but who also feel that weird sense of "now what?"

It's about growing into this new phase without guilt. About exploring who you are outside of snacks and schedules. About creating space for your own joy without abandoning the people you love most.

If you're here, reading this, I want you to know something right up front:

You're not invisible. You're not stuck. You're not broken. You're just in the middle.

And that's where we're going to start.

2

The Weird In-Between

Embracing the Space Between Who You Were and Who You're Becoming

You know what no one tells you about motherhood? That there are these long stretches where nothing is technically wrong, but something still feels...off.

Like: you're not in survival mode anymore. The toddlers aren't melting down over sippy cups. You're not changing anyone's diaper (unless the dog is having a moment). You're not running a carpool. And yet... you don't exactly feel "free."

You look around your house and think, "Okay, great. I finally have two whole hours to myself—laundry is folded, dinner's already planned— so why do I feel like I should be alphabetizing the spices or filing the stacks of paper breeding on every flat surface?"

If I'm feeling good, I might tackle one. If I'm not, I might scroll Instagram or cue up a guilty pleasure show while pretending I don't see the trail of socks leading to the kitchen. And if I've got a book idea rattling around? Forget it—I'm sprinting to the laptop like it's the last slice of cake.

Welcome to the weird in-between.

It's that middle space where your kids are growing up, but not gone. Where you have time, but not energy. Where you could technically reinvent yourself, but you kind of just want to nap.

It's like waking up from a long dream. You blink, look around, and realize you're still in the same pajamas you've had since 2017, and somehow, they still spark joy. Marie Kondo would be proud.

But also? You're not entirely sure where you go from here.

Some days, you get an hour of quiet and panic because you don't know what to do with it. So you scroll your phone, wander to the kitchen, and end up folding laundry that no one asked you to fold just to feel productive.

Other days, you have back-to-back-to-back tasks, and you still feel like nothing got done.

If you're anything like me (and I'm guessing you are, because you picked up this book), this season feels...confusing. You thought you'd feel more by now. More capable. More fulfilled. More on top of things. But mostly, you feel like a browser with 48 tabs open and no idea where the music is coming from.

My kids still need me—but in this weird, arms-length way where I'm somehow both chauffeur and invisible maid.

Let me pause here and ask you a question: Have you ever felt guilty for sitting down?

Not because you were behind on something (although, same), but because it felt like you should be doing something? Cleaning. Prepping. Researching. Building a side hustle. Starting a garden. Learning Mandarin.

Yeah. That guilt? That's not your inner motivation coach. That's capitalism and mom culture having a baby in your brain.

They whisper things like, "If you're not maximizing every moment, you're wasting your life." And we whisper back, "Oh no! I just sat down for five minutes to eat a sandwich —please don't take my mom card."

Here's the truth: this season isn't about becoming a new person. It's about not abandoning the one you already are.

You are someone who:

- Has shown up for your family over and over again, even when it cost you sleep, showers, and probably a few brain cells.
- Has adjusted to physical limitations you didn't ask for, and probably didn't get a user manual for.
- Has figured out homeschooling through sheer will, caffeine, and YouTube tutorials.

- Has supported your household, even when the work came in waves and the laundry came in tsunamis.
- Has scheduled your husband's oil change while chopping potatoes, ordering a Sam's Club pickup, and breaking up a fight about what name the new goldfish should have. Just me?

That's not nothing. That's magic.

This weird in-between season is where a lot of us start feeling like we're malfunctioning. Like something's wrong with us because we're not bursting with passion and drive every morning. Spoiler alert: you're not a robot, and you're not doing it wrong. You're just tired. Emotionally. Mentally. Maybe physically. And maybe spiritually, too.

This is where "embrace the suck" becomes your secret weapon. Not because life is always hard, but because some parts of it are. Awkward transitions. Medical annoyances. Grown-up kids who only need you sometimes. The guilt of not "doing enough," even when you're doing all you can.

We need more honest conversations about this middle place. Where you love your life, but you don't always like your days. Where you're grateful, but also grumpy. Where you're proud of your kids, but also sometimes hide in your car just to finish a podcast.

I notice it in the tired smiles of other homeschool moms with tweens and teens. We look half-awake at co-op drop-off but light up when we get five whole minutes to talk with another adult. We're all running around like unpaid Uber drivers, but underneath it all, we just want someone to say, "Hey. I see you. You're doing great."

So if you feel unsettled, unmotivated, or like you've lost your spark—you're not alone. You're just in the middle.
And the middle is allowed to be messy.

It's the season where growth is happening underground, even when nothing looks impressive above the surface. It's the cocoon stage. (Which, by the way, sounds way more glamorous than it actually is. Cocoons are gooey. Messy. Transformative. Kind of gross. Sound familiar?)

So if today you got out of bed, poured the cereal, answered seven impossible questions, and didn't yell until after 10am, I'm clapping for you. If you did yell before 10am, I'm still clapping for you. (Also, maybe hide the candy wrappers better next time.)

In the next chapter, we're going to talk about what to say when someone asks, "So, what do you do all day?" without crying or punching anything.

But for now, just sit. Sip. Breathe. You're here. And that's enough.

Reflection Questions:

(Jot these down in a journal or let them roll around in your mind while sipping something warm.)

- What's one thing you've done today that you're proud of, no matter how small?

- What's something in your life right now that makes you smile, even on tough days?

Real Life Mom Story:
"That Time I Admitted I Needed a Break (And Took It)"

By Jennie, 35, mom of 3 kids, ages 5, 7, and 11

If someone had told me that admitting I needed a break would be the best decision I ever made, I probably would've rolled my eyes so hard I'd see my own brain.

Mom guilt is a sneaky little monster, especially when you homeschool and feel like you're supposed to do it all — and do it well.

For weeks, I was running on empty. The mornings were a blur of breakfast battles, math lessons, and "Mom! She's looking at me funny!" moments. The afternoons? More of the same, plus laundry mountains that could rival Everest. By bedtime, I was a hollow shell of a person who could barely hold a conversation with my husband without yawning mid-sentence.

One particularly rough Thursday, I found myself hiding in the bathroom (classic move) just to have five minutes of quiet. My 7-year-old was banging on the door, shouting, "Mom! Are you okay?" And that's when it hit me — I wasn't okay. I was burnt out, overwhelmed, and desperately in need of a pause.

But saying it out loud? That was the hard part. "I need a break," I whispered to my husband that night, almost apologizing for even saying it.

His response? "Good. Then take one."

So, I did.

I told my kids we were having a "Mommy Rest Day" (code for, "Don't expect me to be your teacher or referee today"). I called in a friend to watch the little ones for an hour, put on my comfiest pajamas, and curled up with a book I wasn't reading for school. No guilt, no multitasking, just me time.

It wasn't perfect. The laundry was still there. The dishes didn't wash themselves. But my head cleared, my patience came back, and I actually remembered what it felt like to breathe.

The best part? My kids noticed. My 5-year-old gave me an extra hug and said, "Mommy, you look happy."

And honestly, I did.

So here's to admitting when we're overwhelmed, to asking for help, and to taking that well-deserved break — even when mom guilt tries to sneak in. Because we can't pour from an empty cup.

3

So, What Do You Do All Day?

Owning Your Wonderfully Imperfect Daily Life

Some days, my husband comes home and asks, "So, what did you guys do today?"

And I freeze.

Because what did we do?

We didn't go anywhere special. There wasn't a Pinterest craft or a museum outing. Maybe we stayed in pajamas. Maybe we watched a movie just to keep things mellow and manageable. But I feel that familiar flicker of guilt— Was it enough? Should we have done more?

But here's the truth: even on our "mellow" days, my brain was sprinting.

There's the morning rush: reminding kids to log into virtual classes, setting alarms, racing one kid to his math class then the other to her co-op—twenty minutes in opposite directions, both with classes that somehow start at the same time.

Then there's the juggling act: pick up groceries, swing by the pharmacy, squeeze in a doctor appointment for myself. Pick up both kids—dropping one off just in time for her to walk the dog for her dog walking business. Race home, put away groceries, inhale a half-lunch, pack jiu-jitsu bags, and head back out the door. When they're all at jiu-jitsu, I'm doing laundry, washing dishes, and cooking dinner so it's hot when they get home.

It's never just one thing.

I don't get to say, "Well, today I filed reports" or "I finished a project."

I say, "I got everyone fed and where they needed to be, and I remembered to defrost the meat."

And some days, that is a full victory.

What I'm Managing (That You Might Not See)

I'm the mental load manager, scheduler, logistics expert. I remember what groceries we have, what meals work for who, and how everyone's emotional state is trending. I notice when we're out of toothpaste or who's had a rough morning and needs a gentler tone.

I have the kids wash the jiu-jitsu gis right after practice because if we wait, they won't be dry by tomorrow. That little system? That's survival.

I handle our family finances—not just paying bills, but long-term planning, budgeting, and making sure we're on track for security. It's invisible work, but it matters.

I'm the project manager of a household with unpredictable clients and no budget. I'm the IT support for a family network that constantly crashes. I'm the logistics coordinator, therapist, janitor, snack curator, and bedtime negotiator.

And that's on a slow day.

Living in a Body That Can't Do It All

Here's the part that's harder to say out loud: With my Rheumatoid Arthritis, my body doesn't always cooperate.

I can't vacuum the way I want to. I've had to let go of perfection—kids help, but it's not up to my standard. I can't always open jars or reach shelves. I have to ask for help.

There's a pile of Amazon boxes in the corner. I know they need to be opened, unpacked, sorted, flattened—but I literally can't. So I stare at them and wait until someone can help.

This is the mental load that doesn't go in a planner.

This is the invisible weight that builds when you can't just do it yourself.

The Invisible Workload

There's a particular kind of exhaustion that comes from doing a thousand things that are invisible unless they're left undone.

No one congratulates you for refilling the soap dispensers or remembering to RSVP to that thing no one wants to go to. No one throws a parade because you made dentist appointments or scrubbed the mildew out of the shower grout.

But those things? They matter.
They make a home run.
They make a life run.

The Bright Spots: Little Things That Matter More Than They Know

Even in the heaviness, there are sparks.

Like when my kids say, "Thanks, Mom" for a favorite meal, or notice I picked up a special treat just for them. When someone says, "Your kids are so awesome," and I know yes—they really are.

Or when they pause their video game—mid-battle, mid-level—to open a spaghetti jar for me without a word of complaint.

When my husband quietly changes my toothbrush head every morning before leaving for work, because he knows it hurts my arm to do it myself.

These small things? They are giant love letters in disguise.

I'm Still in Here, Too

Sometimes I sit outside with a book and order food I didn't have to cook.

Sometimes I let myself watch sitcoms guilt-free while the kids are at jiu-jitsu with dad.

I could clean. I could "use the time well." But honestly? I just don't wanna.

And that's allowed.

I love to travel. I dream of doing more. But it's tiring now. And there's a part of me wondering: Who will I be when this season ends? What happens when "Mommy" isn't my full-time identity?

I don't have all the answers yet. But I know this: even in the chaos, even when my body can't do it all, I am showing up. I am doing the unseen work. I am loving fiercely.

And that counts.

A Better Answer

You want a real answer to "What do you do all day?"

Okay. I keep humans alive and reasonably healthy. I

educate children who have wildly different learning styles and the attention span of caffeinated squirrels. I maintain a rotating meal plan for people with opinions and preferences that change hourly. I adjust, adapt, and pivot like an Olympic-level emotional gymnast. I make 500 small decisions a day that no one notices unless I get one of them wrong.

You want a business card summary?

"I'm currently managing a multi-level educational facility with a focus on individualized curriculum development, emotional resilience training, and conflict resolution. I also serve as the lead logistics manager, head chef, spiritual advisor, and occasional Uber driver."

Or just:

"I'm doing the kind of work that keeps people alive, sane, and moderately well-fed. It may not make headlines, but it shapes humans. So, you know—no big deal."
Whatever you say, say it with pride. Because there's no bonus check at the end of a long week, no annual review, no fancy name badge—but what you do is real.

You're Doing It Right

You're not failing because your days look like rinse-and-repeat. You're not lazy because you don't have a business card. You're building something sacred: stability, resilience, safety, and love.

Sometimes, you'll crave something beyond motherhood—and that's normal. A project. A creative outlet. Paid work. A new dream.

Other times, you'll just want to be—to sit in the quiet, sip something warm, and not be needed for a full ten minutes.

You're allowed both.

Let that be enough today.

Reflection Questions:

- What's one moment today where you felt truly present with your kids or family?

- What's a small habit or routine that brings a sense of peace or joy to your day?

4

What If I'm Not the Mom I Thought I'd Be?
Letting Go of Old Definitions of Success

There's this idea of motherhood we all carry around, like a little mental movie playing on loop. Sometimes it's drawn from watching our own moms, sometimes stitched together from Pinterest boards, Instagram reels, or those cozy Hallmark movies we binge-watch when no one's looking. Sometimes, it's a picture we painted long before we ever held a baby in our arms—when we still thought we could do it all, all at once, without missing a beat.

For me, I imagined being the mom who was always up for wild adventures with my kids—climbing trees, cannonballing into pools, showing up for every field trip, laughing through spontaneous escapades. My own mom was this incredible whirlwind: a dance teacher who could spin and twirl on the kitchen floor, and a soccer mom who'd jump in to coach when no one else showed up.

I wanted to be just like her—the fun mom with endless energy, showing up big and bold.

But then life had other plans. Right before my kids were born, I was diagnosed with Rheumatoid Arthritis. Suddenly, my body didn't cooperate the way I'd dreamed it would. No more tree climbing, no epic beach games, no jiu-jitsu throws or marathon park days. It felt like the rug was pulled right out from under my expectations.

I remember one day, when my son was little, we went ice skating for the first time. I couldn't even step on the ice with him—not enough strength to hold his hands or catch him if he fell. So, I handed him one of those skate walkers and gave a few tips from the sidelines. Then, I had to let go—literally and figuratively. He skated, stumbled, fell, and got back up all on his own. He came home covered in bruises but glowing with pride, and I realized something important: sometimes, letting go is the greatest gift we can give.

My kids have always loved climbing—trees, walls, boulders—you name it. I couldn't be the mom who climbed alongside them, but I found my role. I became the spotter, the cheerleader, the one shouting foot placements from below. We had one main rule: "If you can get up on your own, you can get down on your own." No rescue missions halfway up the rock wall.

And you know what? They did it. My three-year-old once climbed a two-story rock wall—all focus and determination—and came down safe and sound. That moment taught me something I didn't expect: letting go of my original "mom plan" wasn't a loss—it was a gift. My kids learned independence, confidence, and strength because I believed in them, even when I couldn't do it for them.

I also used to think patience wasn't my strong suit. As a teenager, my younger siblings drove me crazy more often than not. But motherhood? It surprised me with a new kind of patience—one that's creative and quirky. I started explaining things with silly songs or snack metaphors like, "If you have ten cookies, how many would you share with your sister?" I'm not the calm, Zen master or the perfectly organized planner—I'm the mom who turns life lessons into puppet shows and makes the weird work.

I thought I had to be everywhere, doing everything all the time. But my kids showed me that they actually want independence. Sometimes they ask me to watch from the window while they do things their way—no advice, no interruptions. They want me close enough to notice, but far enough to let them grow.

It's so easy to hold ourselves to impossible standards. Did I check all the boxes today? Did I do it gracefully? Did I live up to the "good mom" I imagined? But maybe the better question is: Am I becoming the mom my kids actually need?

Here's the truth: The mom you are right now—tired, learning, adapting, showing up in the middle of the mess —is enough. You are worthy of love, worthy of admiration, worthy of being seen. Even if dinner was frozen waffles, even if the laundry's been in the basket for a week, even if the only thing you conquered today was your own self-doubt.

I thought I'd be out there on the mats, doing jiu-jitsu and tossing my kids around for fun. Instead, I'm the cheerleader on the sidelines, watching them lead projects, look out for younger kids, and Google their way to answers. Their independence speaks louder than any words.

You don't have to be the mom you once pictured. You just have to be you—the real, evolving, beautifully imperfect you. And your kids? They're lucky to have her.

Reflection Questions

- What's one thing you've let go of that you used to think was essential to being a "good mom"?

- What's a surprising strength you've discovered in yourself as a parent?

- How might your limitations have made space for something beautiful to grow?

Real Life Mom Story:
"Not The Mom I Pictured"

By Natasha, 28, mom of 2 kids, ages 4 and 7

I thought I'd be the mom with the chore chart.

The one with the screen-time tokens, the matching water bottles, and the color-coded homeschool folders. I pictured myself floating around the house like some Montessori woodland fairy, hair in a loose braid, offering apple slices and wisdom while classical music played in the background.

Instead... yesterday I fed my kids toaster waffles for dinner. Not homemade ones. The ones from the blue box with the freezer burn on the edges. I scraped syrup off the dog's head and told my four-year-old that yes, cheese sticks counted as vegetables if you squinted.

I used to think I'd be a patient, gentle-voiced "let's talk about your big feelings" kind of mom. But I've actually said the phrase "PUT YOUR PANTS BACK ON" more times than I can count. I yell sometimes. I've hidden in the bathroom with a sleeve of Oreos. I've locked the van doors just to have a moment alone with the music turned all the way up.

I thought I'd love reading aloud every day—oh how I dreamed of reading Charlotte's Web by candlelight,

maybe with tea. But my seven-year-old interrupts every three minutes with a question about pigs, and the four-year-old wants to hold the book herself and inevitably drops it on the baby. (We don't have a baby. She just calls her stuffed possum "the baby.")

And I thought I'd have endless energy. I really did. I imagined crafts, nature walks, baking, themed unit studies. But most afternoons I'm a glorified snack vending machine and referee. The closest we get to themed lessons are the "pirate" paper plates we still have left over from last year's birthday party.

But—here's what I didn't picture, and probably should've.

I didn't picture the way my seven-year-old instinctively reaches for my hand when she's unsure. Or how my four-year-old whispers, "You're my favorite mommy," like there's a whole cast of contenders.

I didn't picture the sound of their giggles from the other room when they make each other laugh. Or the little hand-written note I found yesterday that just said "MOM I LOVE YOU EVEN IF YOUR COFFEE BRETH SMELS."

I'm not the mom I imagined. But I'm theirs.
And I'm exactly the one they need—even in yesterday's hoodie, with hair that hasn't seen a brush since Tuesday.

5

The Myth of Motivation

Why We Don't Need to Be Pumped to Do the Dishes

Let's be honest: if moms only tackled tasks when we felt motivated, half the household would be surviving on granola bars and wearing inside-out socks. Motivation feels great when it shows up, but it's a fleeting, unreliable visitor. We all wait for that spark — that magical internal cheerleader who bursts in with a whistle and clipboard, yelling, "Let's go, ladies! Today's mission: scrub baseboards and meal prep quinoa bowls!" But most days, that cheerleader is nowhere to be found or snoozing somewhere in the back of your brain while you stare at the sink, thinking, Didn't I just do these?

This is why the myth of motivation is so sneaky. It tricks us into believing we have to feel a certain way before we get anything done. And if we don't, it makes us think we're lazy, undisciplined, or broken. The truth is, none of that is true. It just means you're human. What really keeps a house running, a homeschool on track, or a parent showing up for their kids isn't motivation — it's grit, love, and the knowledge that someone is going to ask, "Where's a clean spoon?" at 7 a.m.

I load the dishwasher nearly every night, not because I want to or because some influencer inspired me with perfect bins and color-coded labels. I do it simply because we need dishes tomorrow. That's it. That's the whole reason. Sometimes I don't have the energy to wash every pot and pan, so they soak overnight and wait for another day. Counters stay crusty. Sometimes I'm sore, so I ask one of the kids to finish up. It's not perfect, but it works. This is the rhythm of our life: not Pinterest-perfect, but practical and functional.

Dinner follows the same pattern. Some nights, I have zero energy left. I don't scroll Pinterest, I don't pull out cookbooks, and I don't pretend to be someone I'm not. Instead, I embrace my personal mantra: embrace the suck. Sometimes dinner is cereal, or microwave mac and cheese, or a freezer meal nobody loves but everyone tolerates. Sometimes it's a quirky leftover combo — three chicken nuggets, half a burrito, and some frozen broccoli thrown together. Everyone eats. Everyone lives. That's a win.

My kids get it too. Kitty litter needs scooping every night, or the house smells like a zoo. But if we're out late, they take care of it in the morning. They understand some things just have to get done, even when you don't feel like it. When I'm sore, they jump in to help with dishes and have taken over laundry entirely because it hurts me too much. I don't have to do everything for things to get done.

Some days, I can't wash all the pots, but I can scrub one pan and soak the rest — and that counts. Because waking up to a kitchen that's "clean-ish" makes the next day feel less overwhelming. As for those influencer "motivation hacks," I used to get sucked into the shiny storage containers and rainbow-labeled pantries. Now, I just toss the cereal box into the cabinet, cardboard and all. Nobody's judging me at 7 a.m. — they're just glad there's cereal.

Getting things done isn't always about joy, creativity, or flair. Sometimes, it's simply about doing it anyway. And here's the wild part: the more we release the idea that we have to feel good before we act, the more often we just do the thing — and sometimes, doing it actually helps us feel better. Not magically, not all at once, but enough. Because often, action comes before motivation, not the other way around.

So if you're staring at your to-do list with a blank mind and heavy limbs, give yourself permission to do one small thing — one dish, one email, one kid fed. Then breathe. Then maybe do another thing, or maybe not. You're not broken for needing rest. You're not failing because your energy comes in unpredictable waves. You're adapting, adjusting, showing up — and sometimes, showing up means doing the bare minimum and calling it a win. And guess what? That counts.

Reflection Questions

(Write these down, or just let them percolate while you stir the boxed mac and cheese.)

- What's one task you do consistently—even when you're not in the mood—because it helps future you?

- Are there any responsibilities you could hand off or simplify when your energy is low?

- What's your go-to low-effort dinner or chore survival plan that still gets the job done?

6

Cleaning the House Without Hating Everyone
Small Wins, Big Energy Savers

Let's be honest: if motivation were required to clean a house, most of us would be buried in laundry and eating off paper towels by Tuesday.

And for some of us—especially moms managing a home and a disability—the pressure to keep everything clean and orderly can feel like one more weight to carry. We grow up thinking a clean house equals a good mom, a good wife, a good person. Like if our place doesn't look like our aunt's picture-perfect house with the big yard and spotless surfaces, we must be doing it wrong.

But you know what? That's not true.

Your home doesn't have to be big, spotless, or Pinterest-worthy to be good. It just has to work for the people who live there. And our small condo? When it's "basically clean and good enough for us," I call that a win.

Done > Perfect

Take towels. I love them folded in perfect thirds—tight corners, stacked just so. But perfection takes time and energy, and right now, I need help. The kids or my husband often fold the laundry, and sure, their towel game isn't going to win awards. But guess what? Imperfectly folded towels still dry you off just fine. And letting go of those small standards makes room for something better: shared responsibility.

That's one of the biggest shifts we've made in our house —letting "good enough" be truly enough.

We've spread out the chores because I simply can't do it all. The kids scoop kitty litter, take out the garbage (because, ew, the kitty litter inside), rotate dishwasher duty, and do their own laundry. I usually fold, and everyone puts away their own clothes. It's not always perfect, but it gets done. And that's the goal—not perfection. Just function. Just peace.

Small Tasks, Big Returns

Some days, the mess still overwhelms me. A super messy house stresses me out fast, so I try to break it into small bites. I'll grab a 30-minute timer, rally the family, and we'll tackle as much as we can together. It's not glamorous, but it works.

Sometimes, those small wins bring big energy. Like when the stove gets scrubbed and sparkles? Oh yes. My daughter knows how happy that makes me and will randomly do it just to lift my spirits. That right there is better than a spotless kitchen: it's love in action.

And let's talk about the kitchen for a minute. Ours is tiny —like can't-turn-around-without-bumping-someone tiny. So when it's cluttered or disorganized, it's a huge barrier to getting anything done. That's why it's the one area I'm a little more picky about. It needs to be usable. Period.

It's a Home, Not a Museum

We don't need spotless rooms to be happy. We need paths to the bathroom, clean dishes to eat from, and just enough order to keep life flowing. If I can cover those basics—dishes done, kitty litter scooped, garbage out—I call that a successful day. Sparkles are optional.

Because here's the truth: a little mess means life is happening. And life is way more important than matching throw pillows or towel origami.

Your home isn't a reflection of your worth. It's where you live, recover, grow, and do your best with what you've got. So let the towels be wonky. Let the kids scrub the stove. Let "clean enough" be more than enough.

Because you're doing beautifully—even if the floor isn't vacuumed.

Reflection Questions

(aka: thoughts to chew on while wiping crumbs off the counter):

- Where have I been holding myself to a "perfect" cleaning standard that's stressing me out?

- What small win (like a sparkling stove) gives me a big mental boost?

- Is there something I can delegate—even if it's not done my way?

- Can I give myself permission to stop before perfect?

Real Life Mom Story: "The Text Thread That Never Dies"

By Sarah, 43, homeschool mom of two (ages 13 and 15)

I still remember the day I got added to that group text — a random link passed around at our homeschool coop meet-up. I figured, "Great, another message thread to drown in." But somehow, this one stuck.

It started with a quick question from Megan about science experiments. "Does anyone have a slime-free project? My kids hate goo." Suddenly, replies popped up: recipes for homemade crystals, baking soda volcanoes, even a low-mess leaf chromatography idea. I jumped in, sharing a messy but successful baking soda rocket story from last year. Before I knew it, I was hooked.

That thread became my lifeline. On a hectic Thursday morning when I'm trying to get breakfast into my two teens, pack lunches, and remember which homeschool assignment is due that day, I'd glance at my phone and see a joke about "math homework and teenage eye rolls" from Jenny. Or a photo from Lisa of her kid's science project disaster (complete with exploded vinegar bottle).

One evening, when my kids decided the perfect time to argue was right before bedtime, I quietly slipped away to send a text to the group: "Send coffee and patience, STAT." Within minutes, Megan replied with a virtual coffee emoji and a "You got this!" meme that made me laugh so hard I nearly woke up the whole house.

We don't meet face-to-face much anymore — between coops, lessons, and life, it's tough to coordinate. But those texts? They remind me that I'm not alone in the chaos. They're a little community of moms who get it — the juggling, the imperfect days, the tiny wins.

So if you ever wonder whether those group chats are just noise, remember: sometimes, they're the quiet cheers that get you through the day.

7

Your Kids Are Still Little Enough

The Quiet Magic of Tweens, Teens, and Showing Up Anyway

There's this subtle shift that happens when your kids hit the tween and teen years. One minute, they're climbing into your lap for a bedtime story, and the next, they're texting you from the next room. They're still your kids—still figuring life out—but now with stronger opinions, mood swings, and a phone that practically lives in their hand.

But even as they start pulling away in little ways, they still need us. Not in the same overt, hands-on way they did when they were younger, but in quieter, more layered moments that still mean everything. These years are about learning how to stay close without hovering. It's not always easy, but it's always worth it.

One of my favorite connection tools is the car ride. Something about the lack of eye contact and the hum of the road turns your minivan into a confessional booth. My kids open up about friendship drama, elaborate Minecraft builds, and their latest existential thoughts—all in the ten minutes between home and jiu-jitsu or the store. I've been known to take an extra loop around the block just to keep the conversation going.

Inside jokes and memes have become their own kind of love language, too. We'll send each other random screenshots or videos that don't need any explanation. We're not always saying "I love you," but the message is still there. And that's what this season is really about—finding new ways to say the same old thing: I see you, I care, I'm here.

And then there are the surprises—the moments when something just clicks. Like the Saturday my daughter, unprompted, decided to deep-clean her room. We've asked her for months with no success, and suddenly... she just did it. Not for a reward. Not because I reminded her. Just because something in her brain flipped and said, "Let's do this." It was a glimpse into her growing independence, and honestly, I was floored.

Even our nightly routines have shifted. I used to tell stories and sing songs at bedtime. Now, I help apply zit cream and say goodnight from the hallway. Less cuddly, sure—but still intimate. Still connection. Still love.

As our kids grow, we grow too. Our job isn't to hold onto the exact way things used to be, but to stay present as things evolve. Because they do still need us. Even if they act like they don't.

Reflection Questions:

- How has your connection with your tween/teen changed in the past year?

- What's something small you do just to show them, "I'm here"?

- What parenting habit from the little-kid years has quietly transformed—but still brings you closer?

Real Life Mom Story: "The Day My Teen Actually Asked for Advice (And I Didn't Freak Out)"

By Jessica, 42, Brood: 3 kids, ages 15, 12, and 8

I still remember the exact moment it happened — the moment my fifteen-year-old, usually busy tuning out my "mom lectures" like they were ancient static, actually came to me for advice. Not about homework. Not about snacks. But something... real.

It was a Tuesday afternoon. I was folding laundry, sneaking in a few minutes of silence while the younger two did their math (thank you, homeschool coop), when my oldest, Sam, shuffled into the room with that rare serious look. You know the one: eyebrows slightly furrowed, mouth poised somewhere between "I'm annoyed" and "I'm trying not to cry."

"Mom," he said, hesitating. "Can I ask you something? Like, not about school?"

My heart did that weird jump where you want to celebrate but also panic. "Sure, bud. What's up?"

He perched on the couch, clearly wrestling with how to start. "Well... I've been thinking about college stuff,

and what I want to do, and... I don't know. I guess I'm kinda scared."

Cue all the years of "you'll figure it out" and "take it one step at a time" rehearsed in my brain. But instead, I took a breath and said, "That's okay. I was scared too."

We sat there for a long minute, the kind that stretches just right—not awkward, not rushed. He told me about his worries: what if he picks the wrong path, what if he can't make friends like he does here at home, what if he disappoints me or Dad?

And here's where it got real.

I told him about my own fears—not just as a mom but as a kid who once freaked out about fitting in and picking the "right" thing to do. I admitted I didn't have all the answers. I told him how I'm still figuring stuff out every day.

Then he surprised me by saying, "Thanks, Mom. I just wanted to know you get it."

No eye rolls. No dismissive grunts. Just connection. Later that night, I caught him quietly working on his college list while the rest of us watched a dumb

sitcom. He didn't say much, but I could tell he felt lighter.

Moms, if you're reading this and thinking, "My teen would never come to me," keep showing up. Keep listening. Keep trying to meet them where they are— even when it's uncomfortable. Because sometimes, all it takes is one honest conversation to remind them (and you) that you're on the same team.

And hey, if you can sneak in a laugh or two while you're at it, even better. Like when Sam joked, "So does this mean I can keep asking you stuff, or was this a one-time deal?"

I said, "You've got a lifetime subscription, kid."

8

They Still Need You, Even If They Roll Their Eyes

How to Parent Teens with Humor, Grace, and Memes

Parenting teens isn't about winning every conversation or having all the answers. It's about staying connected through the chaos—with grace, with humor, and, yes, sometimes with memes. These kids may not admit they need us, but trust me: they're paying attention.

I've had full "conversations" with my kids entirely through memes. A single SpongeBob reference or a perfectly timed gif can say, "I see you, I get you, and I'm in this with you." These little exchanges may seem silly, but they're meaningful. They create a bridge between our world and theirs, especially when everything else feels like rules and lectures.

Humor plays a big role here. Playful teasing—done with care—can break tension and build trust. A well-timed "Okay, Miss Bossy-Pants" or a dramatic gasp at their sarcasm says, "I'm not here to control you; I'm here to enjoy you." It creates space for connection in a world where your teen already feels watched and judged from every direction.

And when they show maturity, it's worth acknowledging. One of my kids asked—politely—for five more minutes to finish a show. I didn't launch into a lecture about bedtime routines. I just said, "Sure. Thanks for asking so nicely." That one sentence probably built more trust than a week of parenting pep talks. When we respond with kindness and respect, they learn that independence and cooperation can coexist.

Not every night will be a deep talk. Sometimes they'll hang out in your room and talk your ear off. Other times, they'll offer a quick "Love you" as they disappear into their headphones. But those small things matter. They are connection. They're your new version of bedtime stories and lullabies.

Our teens are balancing hormones, homework, identity, and independence. Some days, they're snarky and moody. Other days, they're insightful and surprisingly sweet. The key is to stay consistent. Keep showing up. Even if the only way in is a shared laugh over a weird anime plot or sitting beside them during a video game you barely understand.

You don't have to do it perfectly. You don't even have to be particularly cool. You just have to be present. One day, they'll look back and realize you were always there—and that matters more than anything else.

Reflection Questions:

- What's one small win you've had with your tween/teen that reminded you, "This is working"?

- When's the last time you made your kid laugh—and what did it do for your connection?

- How are you giving your teen freedom with a safety net?

9

Playdates Aren't Just for Kids

Finding Your People When It's Hard

When I first became a mom, I didn't have a huge village. I had a husband, a baby, and some very sweet and helpful but slightly crazy in-laws. I had one old coworker turned friend I could go to lunch with when my husband came home from work and took over childcare, but I didn't have anyone I could call during the day. No one to call if something weird happened, no one to walk with when I felt stuck or restless. My college and work friends were 3000 miles away and none of them had kids yet. They were kind and encouraging, but their lives were different.

As the kids got older and we started doing gymnastics, swim lessons, and preschool groups, I made a few "class friends." We'd chat during drop-off or sit together in the stands. Some of them even shared goldfish crackers and baby wipes. I got phone numbers and once in a while we'd meet at a park, but usually the friendship ended when the class did. I kept hoping I'd find my "mom tribe," but the real connection I craved just wasn't happening.

I remember one playdate where I thought I had made a real friend. We talked while the kids ran around, and she invited me to coffee. When I showed up, I realized I had walked into a multi-level marketing pitch. I sat awkwardly through a scripted skincare presentation and left feeling embarrassed, disappointed, and a little betrayed. I didn't even want the moisturizer.

Eventually, we moved into a new condo full of other families. My kids had friends to play with and I had other moms to hang out with at the playground. I too became close with one mom. Our kids play together great, even with a large age difference, and we became besties.

We celebrated holidays together, watched each other's kids, and looked forward to our nightly playground "therapy sessions". Our conversations could be deep and raw or silly and absurd. We laughed a lot, and we kept each other sane.

And then they moved. Not far, just far enough that the easy, everyday connection slipped away. Our texts got shorter. Visits took planning. The friendship didn't disappear, but it changed. I grieved what we had, even while being grateful for what remains.

Sometimes we imagine friendship as something magical that just happens. But in real life, it often takes intention, persistence, and a whole lot of awkward beginnings. Especially in motherhood, where our schedules are full and our energy is low, finding and maintaining meaningful friendships can feel like one more thing on the to-do list.

But we need people who see us. Not just in the scheduled playdates or carpool lines, but in the mess, the boredom, the worry, the joy. People who let us be tired or weird or discouraged without needing us to fix it or fake it.

It takes courage to keep looking. To text the mom you only sort of know. To say yes to a walk or invite someone over even if your laundry is piled on the couch. But those small steps are how connection grows—slowly, awkwardly, but beautifully.

Reflection Questions:

- Do you have any "class friends" or acquaintances who might be worth reaching out to for a deeper connection?

- What friendships have changed in your life, and how have you handled the grief that comes with those changes?

- What's one small way you could take a step toward connection this week—reaching out, making space, or just being honest with someone?

Real Life Mom Story: "The Playground That Became a Lifeline"

By Kristi, 38, homeschool mom of four (ages 3, 6, 10, and 13)

If you'd told me before I became a homeschool mom that I'd spend half my week chasing toddlers around the playground while making awkward small talk with strangers, I'd have laughed... and then probably cried.

Between co-op classes, field trips, and juggling four kids ranging from a three-year-old who thinks "sharing" is a mythical concept, to a teenager who lives in her own world, the playground is basically my unofficial office. It's where I get my "me time" — aka watching the chaos unfold while trying not to lose my mind.

That's where I met Gladys. Gladys is a grandma who's about twice my age, but somehow way more energetic and funny than anyone half her age. While I was mentally drafting lesson plans and wondering if anyone remembered to pack snacks, Gladys was cracking jokes about squirrels plotting world domination or how her grandkids apparently believe vegetables are a form of torture.

At first, I figured she'd be bored of me — a sleep-deprived mom in leggings who smells like spilled juice and desperation. But nope. Gladys was a riot, and she never judged the endless snack crumbs in my bag or the fact that I sometimes spoke in toddler gibberish just to keep my youngest entertained.

One day, as my three-year-old launched into an Oscar-worthy meltdown over the slide (because, of course), Gladys leaned over and whispered, "Don't worry, kiddo's just practicing for future drama club." I almost spit out my coffee (okay, water) laughing.

Our chats are never long or scheduled — more like "Hey, did your kid just eat dirt too?" or "Who brought the crazy today?"—but somehow, they keep me sane. Because, honestly, finding a friend who gets it and can joke through the chaos? Priceless.

So, if you're the mom who feels like everyone else already has their crew and you're just the random in the background, keep showing up. Your Gladys might just be hanging out by the sandbox, ready to swap stories and survive this homeschool jungle with you.

10

The Quiet Kind of Lonely

*Why Mom-Friendship Gets Harder
—and What to Do About It*

Sometimes the loneliness of motherhood isn't loud or dramatic. It's just a quiet ache. A slow drift. A realization—somewhere between dropping your teen off at biology lab and texting your kid the Zoom link for creative writing—that it's been a week since you've had a real adult conversation.

You know, one that wasn't about who's bringing snacks to park day or whether anyone's offering Spanish this semester.

Even when we're surrounded by people—our kids, our spouses, fellow homeschool families at co-op—it's possible to feel profoundly alone. Especially when most adult interactions are purely functional:

- "What time does chess club end?"
- "Do we need to submit grades this month?"
- "Is anyone else confused by the group project instructions?"

We long for more than that. We crave real connection. Someone who sees us. Someone who sends a message just to say, "How are you really doing?" Not just "Do you have the syllabus for science?"

Someone who won't blink at the state of our kitchen table or the fact that we kind of lost it during that one math lesson and now we're hiding in the bathroom with a chocolate bar.

But finding that kind of friendship—especially in this season of tweens and teens—is hard.

We see people all the time: in co-op drop-off, during dance class, at the library, the park, the museum, the car. We wave, we nod, we chat about curriculum and class switches. We joke with the grandma who's somehow more stylish and put together than we are. But everyone seems to already have their crew. Their inside jokes. Their long-standing friend group they started when their kids were five.

We do have friends—we text, we share memes, we tag each other in ridiculous homeschool reels. But the deep, soul-filling connection? It's rare. Our bestie from the playground days is still our bestie in theory, but therapy sessions are harder to fit in when we're juggling four schedules and our kids are too old for playdates (but too young to drive themselves anywhere).

Sometimes we finally get a taste of real community. A co-op that clicks. A playdate that turns into something more.

We feel like maybe we've found our place. And then the group shifts, the semester ends, someone moves away, or—worse—everyone else keeps hanging out without us and we wonder if it was us or something else.

It's hard to keep starting over.

Even when we have connections, we can feel lonely. Because some friendships are seasonal. Or surface-level. Or worn thin by life. Or—if we're honest—just draining.

And sometimes, we feel like we're always the outsider. Like the other moms already have their thing. They host book clubs and family dinners and group field trips... and we're over here frantically scanning the group chat, wondering if we missed the invite or if they just didn't think of us.

It's not jealousy. It's just that deep longing to belong.
And friendship in this stage of life doesn't always look how we imagined it. It's not movie nights and spontaneous brunches. It might be texting voice memos while parked at swim team. Or catching up in snippets between pickup and piano. Or a twice-a-semester coffee date that fills your soul in exactly 87 minutes.

It might be one person. It might be five. It might be an online thread where people really get it. But it always starts with honesty. With that one brave sentence:

"I'm kind of lonely."

It takes courage to admit it. To say it out loud. To send the message. To ask, "Want to get coffee?" To let someone into your real life—not just the curated version where everyone's wearing matching t-shirts for the nature walk.

You are not too much. You are not too needy. Wanting connection isn't a sign of weakness—it's a sign of life.

Even if your people haven't shown up yet, it doesn't mean they're not out there. Sometimes they're just waiting for someone else to go first. Sometimes they're sitting two feet away from you at geography class, wondering if you already have a crew.

Keep showing up. Keep reaching out.

You are worth knowing.

Reflection Questions:

- When was the last time you felt seen—not just as a homeschool mom, but as you? What made that moment meaningful?

- Which relationships in your life are draining or one-sided right now? What small boundary or shift might bring relief?

- In this homeschool season, what kind of friendship would feel life-giving? What might connection look like with your current schedule and energy?

- Are there any brave "reach outs" you've been putting off? What's one message you could send today to move toward connection?

Real Life Mom Story: "Date Night That Almost Didn't Happen (But Somehow Did)"

By Laura, 38, homeschool mom of 4 kids, ages 2, 5, 9, and 13

Date nights with my husband used to be these glamorous evenings out—dinner, maybe a movie, some fancy cocktails. But now? Well, let's just say date nights have evolved into a logistical circus with a side of comedy.

It all started when my husband and I decided it was high time to carve out some "us" time. We scheduled a babysitter weeks in advance (hello, homeschool coop moms who save the day!), planned a restaurant that didn't serve chicken nuggets, and even agreed on something to wear that didn't involve yoga pants.

Then came the week of the big night.

Monday: Our toddler decided it was the perfect time to start teething and suddenly develop a fear of sleep. Cue 3 a.m. wake-up calls and a household functioning on coffee and sheer willpower.

Tuesday: The babysitter texted she caught the flu. "Sorry! I can't make it Friday." Panic mode activated.

Wednesday: I spent two hours wrangling the kids for homeschool lessons, during which the 9-year-old spilled juice on the carpet and the 13-year-old declared they "don't do math today" (classic teen rebellion).

Thursday: I had a migraine from the chaos, and my husband was buried in work emails. Date night was looking like a distant dream.

Friday afternoon: Just when I was about to resign myself to a quiet night in, the babysitter called back—her flu test was negative! She was in. Miracle!

Fast forward to 7 p.m.: The sitter arrives, and for the first time in what felt like forever, my husband and I lock the door behind us and walk out without looking back.

We ended up at a cozy little bistro, laughing more than eating because we were so relieved to be out of the house. We reminisced about when date nights meant "staying out past 9 p.m." and giggled over the fact that we still checked our phones every five minutes (mom and dad reflexes, I swear).

On the drive home, we marveled at how rare and wonderful it was just to be together without interruptions. Sure, the date night almost didn't

happen. But when it did? It reminded us why we're in this crazy homeschool, parenthood, marriage thing together.

So here's to the chaotic, imperfect, and absolutely necessary date nights—the ones that almost don't happen but somehow do. Because keeping the spark alive sometimes means laughing through the madness and celebrating the little wins.

11

The Marriage Maintenance Light Is On

Tiny Things That Bring the Spark Back

There's this idea floating around that "keeping the spark alive" means extravagant date nights, second honeymoons, or deeply profound couple's retreats with matching yoga mats. But let's be honest: most of us are just trying to finish our coffee while it's still hot.

Keeping a marriage alive? That usually happens in much smaller, quieter ways—often while half-asleep or elbow-deep in laundry. We've been married for 15 years, together for 21, and I can tell you from experience that spark isn't about candles and champagne. It's about showing up every day, even when the dishwasher's broken and someone's crying in the hallway.

We met in college, at a party I didn't want to go to. My friend dragged me along because she had a crush on a guy there. I wasn't planning to meet anyone. But there he was. He cut his own hair with a number zero buzzer and quickly became my "Baldy." That's still his name, even now, two decades later.

We waited until we graduated and started our careers before walking down the aisle. We weren't rushing into anything. We knew love would be there, but real life needed to come first. And now? Real life is where the love really shows up.

Like this: since my shoulder surgery, changing the toothbrush head hurts my arm. Every morning before work, without me asking, he changes it for me. It's small. But it means everything. It says, "I see you. I want to make your day just a little bit easier."

We still kiss every morning—even if I'm snoring into the pillow and won't remember it. We go to bed at the same time every night, and spoon for a few minutes. Not just for romance, but because it's our quiet way of saying, "Still here. Still us." Even if we're 120 seconds in before one of us peels away and mutters, "Why are you so HOT?"

We send mid-day texts—"Hey sexy" or "I miss you"— usually while one of us is wrestling a toddler or stuck on a call. They don't lead anywhere most of the time. But they remind us we're more than just parents or teammates. We're still those weird college kids who fell in love. Just older. A little achier. Way more into early bedtimes.

Some days are hard. Long work hours. Whining kids. In-laws going off the rails. Pain flares. We've learned not to keep score. No one wins the "Who's More Tired?" Olympics. It just ends in resentment and someone slamming the cabinet too hard.

We've gotten better at naming it instead: "This day was dumb." "We're both exhausted." "Let's press pause."

Then we ask, what's the kindest thing we can do for each other right now? Sometimes that's tacos. Sometimes it's watching something dumb in silence. Sometimes it's switching off with the kids so one of us gets a real shower.

Even on tough days, we try to show up for each other. A kiss. A shared glance. A hug on the couch when I barge in saying, "Watch out, I'm coming in." He always makes space, scoots over, opens his arms. "I'm ruining your situation," I tease. But really, I'm coming home.

We laugh too—especially at night. He makes weird impressions and tells jokes I don't always get. I mix up actors constantly, asking, "Isn't that what's-his-face from the movie with the dog?" He just shakes his head. "That's not even close, bro."

And when it really counts, he shows up. On my 40th birthday cruise, there was a massage special on day one. Without hesitation, he turned to me and said, "You want one?" Then waited in line to get it. Just because.

We don't have rigid rules. We talk through things. We

cuddle often. We know what the other carries—him with work, me with homeschooling and the kids—and we do what we can to make it easier.

It's not about fireworks. It's about maintenance. Quiet loyalty. Flirty texts. Soft touches. The deep knowledge that we're choosing each other again, and again, and again.

Because the goal isn't perfection. It's connection. And maybe making your partner blush at Safeway.

Reflection Questions

- What small, everyday habits keep you and your partner feeling connected?

- How can you both create space for empathy and support when you're equally drained?

- What's one small thing you could do today that would make your partner feel seen or appreciated?

12

Fun Is Not a Luxury

How to Make Joy Part of Your Actual Plan

Here's a wild idea: maybe fun isn't something we reward ourselves with once everything else is finished. Maybe fun is the thing that helps us actually keep going.

Somewhere along the road to adulthood—especially once you add parenting to the mix—joy gets pushed aside. It becomes something optional, something extra, like dessert after the "real" work is done. We tell ourselves we'll get to it after the dishes are loaded, the kids are bathed, the emails are answered, and the laundry is folded. But that moment rarely comes, and the days blur together in a nonstop loop of responsibilities.

But what if joy isn't extra? What if it's actually essential to making the rest of it work?

In our house, fun tends to sneak in during the moments we least expect it—those ordinary, messy, chaotic spaces in between. One morning we were all trying to wrangle the cat, Luna, while heading out the door. Our daughter looked at Luna struggling and casually said, "Yeah, she's a little dumb because she's a second born." We all stopped and stared. Then someone pointed out, "You are a second born!" Her expression was priceless, and we all burst out laughing. That one comment turned into a permanent family joke. Now anytime she does something silly or forgetful, someone says "second born" and the whole house cracks up again.

That's the thing about fun—it often doesn't arrive with a party hat and announcement. It shows up in the middle of the mess, the rush, the repetition. We've learned to let it stay when it knocks.

Music is a big part of that for us. We'll blast "Shut Up and Dance With Me," set a timer, and suddenly the house is alive with noise and motion. Ten-minute sprints of cleaning, dancing, yelling out reminders—whatever it takes to keep things moving without dragging everyone down. It doesn't have to be fancy or well-organized. It just has to be fun enough to cut the tension and make people smile.

Even workouts in our house have a little twist. My husband is a fitness guy, the type who leans toward no-excuses discipline. But that doesn't always fly with the kids. So we've started turning exercise into a game. We'll grab a deck of cards, assign exercises to each suit—hearts mean push-ups, diamonds are jumping jacks—and let the randomness do the work. It's goofy, but it works. They laugh, they move, they stay engaged, and we all walk away without anyone feeling like they were dragged through boot camp.

We also look for small daily rituals to add in connection. Some nights, someone eats late because of practice or work, and even if the rest of us have already had dinner, we'll sit down together and watch a sitcom while they eat. It's not about a big, formal meal—it's about finding a few minutes to feel like a team again, even if we're all on different schedules.

Car rides are their own brand of chaos, but even there we've built in little moments of joy. We joke about who's driving, tease each other about weird habits, and still laugh about the time my daughter, who was about seven, confidently told us all that the UPS trucks were actually Amazon trucks. To this day, we still call them Amazon trucks. It's the kind of inside joke that no one outside the family would get, but it always brings a smile when we see one roll by.

Not every day is light and fun, of course. I get overwhelmed, especially when I'm hormonal or stretched too thin, and I'm not always proud of my reactions. But even in those moments, my husband is usually able to pull me out with a well-timed joke or a ridiculous face. It doesn't solve everything, but it shifts the energy. And sometimes that's all you need to find your footing again.

We believe in fun—not as something to squeeze in after the real stuff, but as part of the real stuff. We get the work done. We show up for our jobs, for our kids, for each other. But we also make space to laugh, to tease, to play. Because life is short. And even when it's not easy, it's still worth enjoying.

Fun doesn't need a vacation or a perfect moment. It just needs a little permission—and a willingness to let it walk in wearing pajamas and making up silly songs while folding laundry.

So make space for it. Not later, not someday, but now. In the chaos, in the in-between, in the actual living. That's where joy belongs.

Reflection Questions

- Where could you create a small pocket of joy this week, even in the middle of your routine?

- What kind of fun do you enjoy—not just your kids? When's the last time you let yourself do it?

- Are there any daily moments (like car rides, chore time, or meals) that could be made more fun with music, jokes, or silly games?

Real Life Mom Story: "The Day I Let Go of the To-Do List (And Rediscovered Fun)"

By Denise, 38, Brood: 4 kids, ages 2, 5, 9, and 13

That Saturday started like most others — the toddler decided to use the cat as her personal canvas (sorry, Whiskers), the 9-year-old was already bored before breakfast, and my teenager was deep into scrolling through her phone like it was a lifeline.

I was drowning in a mental checklist: homeschool lessons to prep, laundry piling up, dinner plans floating somewhere in the back of my brain. And then, I just stopped. No more chasing my tail trying to check every box.

"Let's have a no-agenda day," I announced, mostly to myself but loud enough for the kids to hear. They looked at me like I'd lost my mind. The teenager rolled her eyes but said, "Fine, whatever." The 9-year-old gave a hopeful smile, and the toddler clapped like I'd just announced ice cream for breakfast.

By noon, our living room was a fortress of blankets and couch cushions. Popcorn became lunch

(because who can build a fort and eat broccoli at the same time?). We danced to ridiculous songs and laughed until the walls echoed.

Whiskers, the newly decorated feline, gave me the kind of judgmental stare only a cat can master, but even he seemed to settle down.

That day, the to-do list didn't exist. The laundry could wait. The books didn't need reading. Instead, we just showed up, silly and messy and perfectly imperfect.

And honestly? I went to bed feeling a little lighter than I had in weeks.

13

Purpose Doesn't Have to Be Productive

You Matter Even If You Never "Start a Business"

There's this sneaky little lie so many of us accidentally believe: that unless you're building something, launching something, or monetizing something, you're somehow wasting your life.

We don't say it out loud, but it echoes in our heads every time we scroll past someone announcing their new business or side hustle or perfectly organized home office. It's the cult of productivity—and it doesn't show up in a creepy robe. It shows up in yoga pants, holding a planner and whispering, "You've got the same 24 hours as Beyoncé." "You should totally turn that hobby into passive income." "If you rest now, you'll fall behind."

But let me say this as clearly as I can:
 You are not a brand.
 You are not a walking TED Talk.
 You are not a machine built for output.

You're a human being—with a soul, a body, and a life that matters even when nothing gets checked off the to-do list. Even when the dishes sit in the sink, the emails go unanswered, and you forget what day the library books are due.

I know what it's like to want to do more. I work part-time doing real estate showings, and I write books in the margins of the day. I carry dreams—big ones. I want to build something that gives my family breathing room, that maybe lets my husband retire sooner. I want our life to feel lighter.

But my body doesn't always cooperate. Some days I physically can't clean the whole house or write another chapter or take on more work. And it's frustrating. Because my brain is full of ambition, but my energy runs out before I get through half the list.

So when I say I see you, I mean it.

And here's what I've learned the hard way: Just because you can push yourself harder doesn't mean you should. Sometimes what you really need isn't another idea or project or 7-step monetization strategy. Sometimes you just need... a nap. A long shower. A cookie you don't share. An episode of that bingeable show you've been saving. That's not laziness. That's being human.

Now, if you want to start a business? Please do. Open the Etsy shop. Launch the coaching group. Sell your watercolor pet portraits or your sourdough starter kits.

Let your creativity bloom. But don't do it because you think you have to prove your worth. Don't do it because Instagram told you rest is for the unmotivated. And don't do it because someone else's highlight reel made you doubt the goodness of your own life.

Your purpose isn't measured by income streams. If your family is safe, fed, and has some leftovers in the fridge— that's not failure. That's grace. That's enough.

Honestly, sometimes I look around at my house and feel overwhelmed by what I can't do. But then I remember what I can. When a friend of mine was in the hospital for over a week, I was able to pick up her kids from school, help with homework, make them dinner, and keep them company until their dad could come home. I was tired.

But I was also so grateful—to have the freedom in my schedule to show up like that. That's purpose. It's not flashy or scalable. But it's real.

Purpose might look like folding laundry while praying for peace.

 It might look like laughing with your spouse over takeout and a silly movie.

It might be listening—really listening—as your teen explains something in Minecraft you don't understand at all.

 It might be choosing to rest even when the laundry isn't done and the house is still a mess.

It's radical to believe your worth isn't tied to your productivity. But I promise you, if today all you did was keep your people warm, fed, and emotionally intact? You did enough. You are enough.

Reflection Questions

- What invisible work do you do that keeps your family running smoothly?

- If you had no pressure to earn or prove anything, what would you enjoy doing just for yourself?

- How can you give yourself permission to rest without guilt?

14

Part-Time Jobs, Full-Time Dreams

Making Space For Things That Excite You

There's this strange pressure that settles on many parents once they have kids—a pressure to pick a single lane and stay there forever. You're either the career-driven mom or dad who climbs the corporate ladder, schedules daycare down to the minute, and never misses a deadline, or you're the full-time, Pinterest-perfect, sourdough-baking, sensory-bin-making parent who lives entirely in the world of snack schedules and laundry piles. But what if you don't fit neatly into either of these boxes? What if you're somewhere in between?

Maybe you enjoy working, but only some of the time. Maybe you don't want the full-time grind, but you also want more than just managing the household chores and the kids' endless activities. That middle ground—the space where part-time work meets full-time parenting—matters. It's important. It might be a part-time job that keeps your brain engaged or a side hustle that sparks a flicker in your soul, even if it's not a roaring bonfire yet. Whatever it is, you are absolutely allowed to have dreams. Big dreams, tiny ones, or half-finished plans tucked away in notebooks or buried on your computer in a folder labeled "Someday." Whether you're working full-time, part-time, or juggling the overwhelming feeling of no-time-for-anything, it's powerful and important to do something simply because it makes you feel alive.

For me, that something has always been real estate. Since high school, I've been drawn to it—the idea of fresh starts, new kitchens, the moment someone walks into a house and knows it's theirs. When I became a stay-at-home mom, I got my real estate license, not to dive into a full-time career but to find a way to be part of something exciting without overwhelming myself. Now, I work part-time as a showing assistant. I get to do only the fun parts: meeting people, exploring houses (yes, I'm a little bit of a snoop), and getting paid for it. It fits my life, my energy levels, and my schedule perfectly.

I've tried other ventures too. I ran a personal finance blog for over two years, and while I loved sharing my knowledge—people told me it helped them tremendously —it ended up costing me more in time, stress, and money than it ever earned. It brought in maybe $50 a year, but took hours of work every week and even cost a few hundred dollars to keep up. Eventually, I had to let it go. That was tough, but I don't regret it. Trying something and discovering it's not the right fit is still growth. It reminded me that it's okay to explore, to start something, and to walk away if it's no longer serving you.

What I really want—what so many of us want—is something that feels like our own. Not a full-time all-consuming career, but a part-time spark that makes us feel creative, engaged, and more like ourselves. I don't need perfection or massive success; I just want to feel alive in small ways that remind me I'm still here beyond the everyday mom tasks. I've learned that it's okay to try things, to make mistakes, and to change course. That kind of freedom is a gift.

At the same time, I've learned the hard way that trying to juggle too many things is a fast track to burnout—and a guaranteed way to let the laundry pile up and judge you from across the room. Believe me, I know. You don't have to turn every passion into a business plan. You can love something quietly, without pressure or Instagram followers. The way you live your life teaches your kids far more than chores or manners. You show them what it means to be curious, to try new things, to not have it all figured out, and still find joy.

Your identity does not disappear once your kids outgrow their footie pajamas. You are still in there. Your spark is still glowing, even if it's buried beneath a mountain of to-dos right now. So if folding towels is the only quiet moment you've had all day, let that be your reminder: You are allowed to dream. And, just as importantly, you are allowed to rest.

Reflection Questions

- What activity or interest makes you feel like you again —even if it's only for 10 minutes?

- Is there a hobby or side hustle you've wanted to explore but felt guilty about starting? What if you gave yourself permission?

- What can you let go of so that you have more energy for the things that give you life?

Real Life Mom Story: "The Day I Tried to Be CEO, Chef, and Chauffeur All at Once (And Realized I'm Only Human)"

By Megan, 41, Mom of 3 kids, ages 4, 8, and 14

I've been running my handmade candle business for about a year now. It started as a little side hobby—making candles in the evenings after the kids were asleep. I loved it so much that last year, I decided to officially launch an online shop, and now I'm slowly trying to grow it into something more. My plan is to eventually have a steady stream of custom orders, plus wholesale accounts with local shops. But for now, it's baby steps—posting on Instagram, packing orders between school drop-offs, and squeezing in some candle-making whenever I can.

This morning, I set out to do a few important things: respond to emails from customers, create a new scent blend to test, and schedule some posts for the week. Nothing huge, just steady progress.

But of course, the house had its own agenda.

The four-year-old started asking for snacks the second I opened my laptop. The eight-year-old wanted help with a math problem (which I'm definitely out of

practice on), and the teen needed a ride to choir rehearsal—right when I was mixing wax and trying not to spill it everywhere.

I tried to multitask—typing a quick reply while handing over goldfish crackers, stirring wax while negotiating who got the last cup of juice—but by noon, my carefully planned to-do list was scattered all over the kitchen table alongside sticky fingerprints and Lego pieces.

It's frustrating sometimes. The house is loud. The chaos is constant. But I've learned not to expect long stretches of focused work anymore. Instead, I break my goals into tiny, manageable bites. Ten minutes here, five minutes there. Some days I barely get to it, and that's okay.

The candles aren't going anywhere, and neither am I. I remind myself that growing a business and being a mom is a marathon, not a sprint. It's okay if my "office" is in the middle of a messy kitchen, and if my plans don't happen on my schedule. Every little progress—posting that Instagram photo, packing one order, testing a scent—adds up.

So yeah, the house will be crazy tomorrow, and the day after, and the day after that. But I'll keep lighting my little candle, one flicker at a time.

15

You're Allowed to Be Tired and Still Magical

Showing Up With Love (And Maybe a Little Dark Chocolate)

Some days, you're crushing it. Other days, it feels like life is rolling over you in a minivan full of laundry and to-do lists. Most days? You're just plain tired. Not "I stayed up too late watching baking shows" tired—more like "I've made 74 micro-decisions before 9 a.m." tired. It's the kind of tired that lives in your bones, that makes your brain hum even when your body's still. But somehow, even in that state, you're still doing an incredible job.

There's this weird pressure to feel guilty for being tired, like if you just had better systems or more motivation, you wouldn't feel this way. But let's be honest: it's not laziness —it's life.

You're the emotional, logistical, and nutritional epicenter of your family. You are coordinating who needs snacks, who's out of socks, who has that appointment tomorrow, and whether dinner involves real vegetables or just cereal. You might be sitting behind the wheel all day, chauffeuring kids from one place to another, but your mind? It never stops moving.

And yet, even when you're running on fumes, you still show up. Maybe not with a Pinterest-worthy project or a fresh loaf of sourdough, but you show up with presence. With care. With love. Sometimes that looks like dragging yourself to the couch and tossing out dinner ideas while your people raid the fridge. (Because even when your body's down, your brain still shows up for your family.) Sometimes it's just walking over, handing a jar to your husband with a quiet "help please," and knowing he'll take it from there with a smile.

We think being tired means we're not doing enough. But what if it means we've done a whole lot already?
You don't need to hustle your way to being "enough." You already are. On some days, love looks like warm meals and patient lessons. On others, it looks like a frozen pizza and calling dibs on the corner spot of the couch. Either way? You showed up. You cared. And that counts.

If you need a break, take it. One of my favorite things to do when I feel myself hitting that wall is to grab a piece of dark chocolate, lie down for five solid minutes, and just... do nothing. No scrolling, no talking, no planning. Just quiet. And somehow, that tiny pause helps me get back up and keep going.

It's okay to say, "I need a moment." That moment might be a quick nap, a bathroom break with your favorite phone game, or five minutes of silence where no one asks you for a snack. Whatever it is, you're allowed to take it without guilt. Your family doesn't need a perfectly productive martyr. They need a present, honest human who knows when she's done and says so.

And when that moment isn't enough, tag in your team. Let the kids make their own sandwiches. Let your spouse handle bedtime. Announce, "Dinner is not me tonight," and call it a win. In our house, we pass the baton when someone's running low. There are no trophies for burning out over who folded the towels.

The guilt loves to whisper that we're not doing enough.

But here's the reality:

Your kids are still learning and growing.
Your partner still laughs with you over late-night cereal.
Your friends still text, even if you forget to respond for a week.
You're still the one they all look to for comfort, support, and leadership—even when you're lying on the couch, eyes half-closed, offering meal ideas with one hand and shielding your chocolate stash with the other.

So here's the truth:

You can rest and still be strong.
You can pause and still be present.
You can be exhausted and still be magical.
Magic isn't always glitter and glow-ups. Sometimes it's breathing through the chaos. Sometimes it's whispering "I

need a moment" instead of screaming. Sometimes it's smiling through a headache or loving your people from the quiet corner of the room. That's not weakness. That's grace.

You don't need a productivity tracker to prove your worth. Your love, your presence, your effort—even when tired—is more than enough.

Reflection Questions:

- When was the last time you gave yourself credit for something small that felt big?

- Who shows up for you, and how can you let them help a little more often?

- What's one sign that—even when you feel like you're falling short—your kids, partner, or friends are still thriving?

16

What If This Is Enough?
Peace, Presence, and Putting Down the Pressure

We live in a world that's obsessed with more.

More hustle. More achievement. More side income. More Pinterest-perfect family calendars where each child is thriving in jiu-jitsu, building apps, and singing soprano in a traveling youth choir.

And sure—growth has its place. But sometimes, I look around at our life and think, What if this is enough?

Right now, we're in a really peaceful chapter. Not the flashy kind that gets attention on social media. The quiet, cozy kind you almost don't notice until you realize how rare it is.

Most days, my husband heads off to work, and I wake up around 7am—rested, which already feels like winning. I stretch, read a little, then wake the kids and make a real breakfast. Yes, eggs and toast. Nothing fancy, but something warm to start the day right.

need a moment" instead of screaming. Sometimes it's smiling through a headache or loving your people from the quiet corner of the room. That's not weakness. That's grace.

You don't need a productivity tracker to prove your worth. Your love, your presence, your effort—even when tired—is more than enough.

From there, we're off to whatever class or volunteer activity is on the schedule, or the kids dive into homework. In the afternoons, my husband and kids all head to jiu-jitsu (it's like a second home at this point), and I get a few hours to tidy up, cook dinner, write—or, let's be honest, watch a couple episodes of my current binge-worthy show. Then we regroup for dinner, often shared over our favorite show, a little messy but very us.

Evenings are simple. Quick house reset: I do the dishes, my daughter tackles the kitty litter, my son takes out the trash, and the jiu-jitsu gis get washed and hung. Everyone gets a little time to themselves. The kids unwind with a game or anime, and my husband and I talk, scroll, or—ahem—enjoy the kind of connection that doesn't get discussed at the dinner table. Then it's lights out. Sleep comes easy when your days are steady.

It's not all ease, of course. My husband's had some hard years at his job. It's not his dream gig, and some days wear him thin. But it provides excellent benefits, which is huge with my medical condition. He gets lots of time off, golfs often, and still makes it home in time to take the kids to train and get some training in himself. And when he's worn down? He still shows up.

I used to think success meant big milestones. Home ownership. Building a business. Investing in a rental property. And then I realized: we are investing—just not in the Instagram way. Renting in a high-cost area actually saves us a ton. We're close to everything. No commutes. No big maintenance costs. Just a small space that's easy to clean, easy to afford, and lets us say yes to the things we actually value.

Take last weekend. My husband wanted to hit the golf range, and even though I usually stay home, I went along. I can't swing a club (my joints said "absolutely not"), but he brought me a folding chair, we stopped for bubble tea, and I sat in the shade sipping while he practiced. We laughed. We talked. Then we drove the five minutes back home—and the kids had already made dessert and finished their homework. It was the simplest day, and I kept thinking, This. This right here.

I talk to other moms whose lives are overflowing with activities and expectations, and I get it. Life pulls hard sometimes. But I also look around and see what we've built—something steady, kind, and even joyful. Not perfect, but peaceful.

It's easy to feel like I should be doing more. Shouldn't I want to scale something, create more streams of income, enroll the kids in elite camps, or at least own something big? But I come back to our life and see something better than ambition: presence. Flexibility. Freedom. We have savings. Low stress. Time together. The ability to shift plans when someone needs us. And that, to me, feels like real success.

It may not look flashy. But I know this:

It's enough.

Actually, it's more than enough.

Reflection Questions:

- What does "enough" look like in your life right now?

- What small moments or routines bring you peace, even if they wouldn't make it into a highlight reel?

- Who contributes to your sense of stability and contentment—and how can you let them know they matter this week?

Conclusion

Still You. Still Worthy. Still Here.

If you've made it to the end of this book, I'm guessing it wasn't with candles lit and a warm cup of tea in peace and silence. More likely, you were sneaking in a few paragraphs between appointments, throwing together dinner, or collapsing on the couch with someone asking, "What's for breakfast tomorrow?" while you're still wiping down the counter from tonight.

But you made it here. And that counts for something.

My hope is that you're not closing this book with a longer to-do list, but with a softer perspective. A reminder that you're not behind, broken, or barely hanging on—you're a human raising humans. You're navigating bodies in motion, moods in flux, and somehow, amidst it all, you're creating a life that's not just surviving—but sometimes, in flashes, truly beautiful.

Not because you've figured it all out. Some days, your

house might look like a tornado hit it. Some days, dinner's just leftovers in a tortilla, and that's still a win. (Actually, those pulled pork burritos were so good they felt restaurant-worthy—and everyone agreed.) Some days, you skip the activity you planned because your daughter's cramping and miserable, and instead, you curl up together with tea and frozen blueberries and look up ways to soothe the pain. That's not a failure of your schedule—it's a picture of motherhood done well.

This journey was never about becoming someone else. It's about learning to be you, with a little more grace. The version of you who gets tired, who fields a dozen interruptions an hour, who scrubs the bathroom when your body would rather collapse, who deals with all the background noise of "he's touching me" and "you sound like Grandma," and still shows up again tomorrow.

You don't need to hustle harder or optimize your productivity app. You need to be allowed to be. To recognize that this stage of life is full and loud and chaotic, yes—but it's also full of moments that are rich and grounding. Like your daughter working on a new art project, fully immersed in creating something just for you. Or the quiet of the whole house after dinner, when everyone's finally content and the conversation turns silly or unexpectedly deep.

There's wisdom in the way you've adapted. In how you've stopped letting extended family drama live rent-free in your mind. In how you've come to accept your version of being a "playful mom" doesn't require running around outside—it can be a good joke, a silly face, a shared meme, or just showing up ready to listen. You've learned to let go of some of the pressure and lean into presence instead. That's growth. That's enough.

And while no one's clapping when you fold laundry or restock the toilet paper or get the jiu jitsu gis in the wash for the next day, I see you. This whole book has been a nod to that unseen labor. To the things you carry, the things you care about, and the way you love your people even when you're running on fumes.

So if you needed someone to say it, here it is: you're doing better than you think. You don't have to earn rest. You don't have to be in constant motion to be a good mom. You don't have to keep up with anyone else's life to feel proud of your own.

You're still you. Still worthy. Still here.

And we're all better for it.

P.S.

If this book made you smile, nod your head, or maybe even say, "Yep, that's totally me," I'd love it if you shared it with a fellow parent who's juggling a million things right now. You know—the one surviving on coffee, random snacks from couch cushions, and sheer determination.
They might need this gentle reminder as much as you did.

And hey, if you have a minute (or the time it takes your kid to brush their teeth while singing their favorite song on repeat), leaving a quick review would mean the world to me. Just a few honest words about how this book landed for you can help someone else find it—and feel a little less alone in the chaos.

Thank you for being here, for reading, and for showing up in your own wonderfully imperfect way every single day. You made it through to the end, and that deserves a big virtual high-five (and maybe a secret piece of dark chocolate too).

Keep going at your own pace. You're enough. You're doing better than you think. And you are absolutely worthy of rest, laughter, and all the messy, beautiful moments in between.